AMERICAN ESSA

SERIES EDITOR,

PLACES FOR WORSHIP

A Guide to
Building and Renovating

MARCHITA B. MAUCK

THE LITURGICAL PRESS
Collegeville, Minnesota

1	2	3	4	5	6	7	8	9

Library of Congress Cataloging-in-Publication Data

Mauck, Marchita.
    Places for worship : a guide to building and renovating / Marchita
      Mauck.
        p.   cm. — (American essays in liturgy)
    Includes bibliographical references.
    ISBN 0-8146-2283-6
    1. Liturgy and architecture—United States. 2. Church facilities-
-Planning. 3. Church committees—Catholic Church. 4. Churches,
Catholic—United States. 5. Catholic Church—Liturgy. I. Title.
II. Series: American essays in liturgy (Collegeville, Minn.)
BX1970.3.M38 1995
246'.9582—dc20   94-7252
                                                    CIP

Contents

Introduction   7

   A. What Kind of Place Do We Need?   9

   B. How Do We Approach a Building or
      Renovation Project?   10

   C. Where Do We Begin?   11

1 Preliminary Preparation   13

   A. The Formation of a Committee   13

     1. Mandate for Decision Making   13

     2. Credibility   13

   B. The Development (or Refinement) of a
      Parish Mission Statement   14

   C. The Assessment of Parish Physical Resources   16

   D. Assessment of Financial Capabilities   17

2 Selection of a Liturgical Consultant   18

   A. Do We Need One?   18

   B. What Does a Liturgical Consultant Do?   18

   C. Where Do We Find a Liturgical Consultant?   20

   D. How Do We Interview Liturgical Consultants?   22

   E. How Much Will the Services of a
      Liturgical Consultant Cost?   23

3 Selection of an Architect   25

   A. How Do We Find Architects
      Who Might Be Interested in Our Project?   25

   B. Setting Up the Interviews   26

C. What Are the Principles for Interviewing Architects?   27
D. How Do We Make a Choice of the
    Candidates We Have Interviewed?   28
E. What Is Involved in Identifying the
    Architectural Services We Need?   28
F. How Much Will Architectural Services Cost?   32

4 Getting Down to Work   33
  A. Pre-Design and Programming   33
    1. Work with the Architect   34
    2. Work with the Planning Committee   35
      a. Hospitality of Site   35
      b. Portal/Entry/Threshold   36
      c. Baptism   37
      d. Reconciliation (Penance)   41
      e. Eucharist   42
      f. Consideration of Other Rites   45
      g. Reserved Eucharist   50
      h. Devotional Images   52
    3. Work with the Assembly   54
      a. Advisory Committees   55
      b. The Community's History   55
      c. Liturgical Formation   55
  B. Master Site Plan   59
    1. Architect   59
    2. Parish Planning Committee   59
    3. Assembly   60
  C. Schematic Design   60
    1. Architect   60
    2. Parish Planning Committee   61
    3. Assembly   61
  D. Design Development   61
    1. Architect   61
    2. Parish Planning Committee   61
    3. Assembly   63
  E. Construction Documents   63
  F. Construction   64
    1. Architect   64
    2. Parish Planning Committee   64

    a. Working with Artists   64
    b. Planning for the Rite of Dedication   65
  G. Post-Construction Reflection
    on the New Worship Space   65

5 Worship Places with Special Needs   66
  A. Cathedrals   66
  B. Catholic Health Care Facilities   68
  C. Chapels for Religious Communities   69
  D. University Newman Centers or Student Chapels   70

Introduction

Building or renovating places for worship can be both exciting and agonizing. Before anything is set to paper, one needs to understand the motivation behind the endeavor. It is naive to believe that building or renovating a church is merely about crafting a beautiful worship space. It is rather about translating a liturgical theology (i.e., what we believe about what we do in ritual actions) and beauty into three dimensions. It is about forming a holy people whose lives are transformed, motivated, formed, and sustained by their experiences in that place.

The faith of the assembly is shaped and celebrated in the rituals of initiation into the community's life. The rituals of reincorporation and reconciliation follow periods of absence, sin, and alienation. The mission of both Christ and the assembly is found in the celebration of the Eucharist, in the marrying and burying and anointing and praying that make up the Church's shared life. It is the celebration of rites that determines the design of a space for worship. It is the celebration of rites that constitutes the on-going identity of Christians, an identity ever strengthened by the days, seasons, and events of the lives of the faithful who gather there year after year.

These rites of being born and dying and rising, of washing and anointing, of eating and drinking demand *ritual places*. Ritual places are those which confront the faithful with the risks and consequences of a transforming relationship with God. It is not enough to have a thrust-stage sanctuary and semi-circular seating in order to have a good ritual space for the Eucharist. It is not enough to have a baptismal font that holds lots of water in the midst of the assembly (but in the wrong place) to meet the demands of the rites of initiation. It is not enough to have elegant living room furniture in the place where penance is celebrated if that place is reminiscent of a counselor's office and located next to the restrooms. Unless there is the opportunity for taking the risk of death itself by plunging into the living waters of baptism, the ritual place for baptism remains ineffective. Unless there is the opportunity for the whole assembly during the night watch of the Easter Vigil to enter into the mystery of regeneration in life-giving waters at a ritual place that presumes their presence is intentional, then the baptismal place reflects private celebration of baptism. A ritual place for the celebration of reconciliation without any relationship to the font and the first forgiveness of sins commits a gross oversight of our history and tradition regarding penance and baptism. If all our efforts at building or renovating churches are merely exercises in tasteful interior decoration, we may end up with beautiful buildings, but miss the point.

My concern in this essay is to demonstrate that worship spaces are places for a variety of ritual actions involving the whole assembly and multiple ministries. Therefore, the process for designing these spaces must proceed from the ritual demands of the assembly at worship. We are only thirty years into the reforms of the Second Vatican Council. We have just completed our first generation of response to these reforms. Now, at the beginning of the second era of reflection about our worship, we realize that the primary concern is the celebration of rites rather than the arrangement of furniture and the visibility of the altar. For example, in the rites of Christian initiation, the ritual spaces of threshold (portal), font, and table become critical *loci* of liturgical action. The worship space must reflect a sensitivity to "outside" and "inside" for the rite of acceptance and enable a crossing of the threshold into the life of the community. The Easter Vigil requires ritual space at the font to accommodate the entire assembly around it as a "company of holy witnesses." The design and shape of the font itself must speak of the theology of descending into the grave to raise up a new creation in Christ. The placement and centrality of the table in relationship to this font should speak the bipolar centrality of baptism and the Eucharist to the life of this community.

What makes of these places "ritual places"? These are the places where the whole assembly converges to do the work of Christ and celebrate the mysteries of faith.

A. What Kind of Place Do We Need?

The United States bishops' document *Environment and Art in Catholic Worship* (1978) (EACW)[1] describes the building that houses the Church as a "skin" that wraps around the place where worship occurs (n. 42). This is an interesting analogy, suggesting that what is most important is not the structure, which is more like an encompassing membrane, but the activity which is embraced by the structure. Rarely do buildings transform lives. But buildings can invite the kind of experiences that transform lives. Such a vision implies that when reflecting upon design solutions one begins with what occurs inside or in relationship to the building designed for worship.

EACW describes the gathered assembly of believers as the primary symbol of the liturgy (n. 28). This of course implies that it is the holy actions of the assembly that constitute the symbolic language of worship—not the "things" such as altar, ambo, font, cross, tabernacle. Those "things" are important insofar as they become the focal point for an activity.

To speak in this way is to say that the purpose of the church building is to support and nurture the spiritual life of the assembly. It is the locus of ongoing formation of the community's Christian life together. Thus we use verbs to talk about the building. It "supports" and it "nurtures" precisely by offering the quality of space that will invite the assembly to do what it most needs to do. And when the assembly does what it needs to do, we then speak of the *ritual places* where these actions occur.

The place for worship is shaped by the Christian journey of the believers who assemble there. There is a resonance between the sequence by which we celebrate sacraments and the rhythms of human life. Since the beginning of life in the community is celebrated by baptism, it is appropriate to envision the place for the celebration of our entry rite(s) (baptism and reconciliation) as located near the entrance of the building itself. It is likewise appropriate to imagine some distance between the font (and by extension the reconciliation chapel) and the altar signifying the journey that is made from one to the other, from baptism to the Eucharist. In this way baptism and the Eucharist can continue to be experienced as the two sacraments around which all the others revolve. Envisioning the baptismal font with its flowing water and the altar as anchors for *places*

---

[1] *Environment and Art in Catholic Worship*, National Conference of Catholic Bishops' Committee on the Liturgy (Chicago: Liturgy Training Publications) 1990.

at which the assembly gathers for a whole variety of ritual purposes frees the imagination for considering all the additional ways in which the entire assembly of able people and people with disabilities might encounter the holy, which changes their lives. The breadth of one's vision of worship determines the effectiveness of the design solutions in meeting the worship needs of the community.

Places of worship that succeed in drawing people into transformative experiences will always respect the power of symbol. This means that they will be hospitable and inviting. They will express a reverence for the created world and the materials which are used. The appointments and liturgical items will be beautiful and appropriate in form and scale and designed specifically for inviting the assembly to enter more fully into the mystery to which they refer. Such places of worship will respect the sacredness of human experience, and attend to the needs for primarily active corporate worship as well as for more contemplative and personal devotional opportunities.

B. How Do We Approach a Building or Renovation Project?

A building or renovation project is more than a construction job. It is an opportunity for building and renewing the community as well. The amount of time, energy, and financial resources required for building or renovating a place of worship is so great that such an undertaking occurs only once every several generations. Responsible stewardship demands that the community take advantage of such an opportunity and renew its commitment to the life of the community and all that sustains it. This calls for reflection on the identity and mission of the assembly and ownership of the mission and its expression in the new or renewed place for worship.

How does that ownership evolve? If the language of the process is that of the spiritual formation of the assembly, of the shared journey of faith in which all participate, then the community grows as the process unfolds. The formation of the assembly is not the same as "adult education." The process is not one of classroom lectures or of religious catechesis. Rather the building process becomes an occasion for the community to reflect upon the rites it celebrates as the foundation for understanding its identity and mission. The journey of faith of a particular community—considered in the context of our traditions and the contemporary challenges of the Church and its rites—is the focal point of any building or renovation process.

C. Where Do We Begin?

A basic sequence of events for a successful building project might be:

1. Form a building or renovation planning committee and define its responsibilities.
2. Select a liturgical consultant.
3. Select an architect.
4. With the liturgical consultant and architect, begin a formation process for the planning committee and the larger parish as the foundation for the "programming" phase.
5. Develop a master site plan.
6. Proceed with the "design" phases of the project.
7. Follow diocesan guidelines for approval of plans, fund-raising, bidding process, and construction contracts.
8. Begin construction.
9. Prepare a ritual "leave-taking" for the community's departure for renovation and construction, and a Rite of Dedication for the completed worship space.

Some of these events will overlap in the course of the project. The following chapters will explore these and related topics.

1 Preliminary Preparation

A. The Formation of a Committee

The two most critical requirements for an effective building/renovation committee are an official mandate for decision making from the parish and credibility.

1. Mandate for Decision Making

The official establishment of the building/renovation committee ideally originates as a recommendation of the parish council to the pastor who concurs. In this way, through its elected representatives, the parish claims ownership of the project from the beginning. This implies not only ownership of the physical plant, for which they will be paying, but also a commitment to the faith community and the quality of their spiritual journey.

The charter establishing the building/renovation committee should clearly outline its responsibilities. Clarity concerning the responsibilities enables members to know the nature of the commitment they are being asked to make and enables the committee to stay on track during the project. This responsibility is threefold:

  a. to initiate and carry through a systematic assessment of liturgical, practical, and spatial needs,
  b. to arrive at design solutions to meet those needs, and
  c. to make recommendations through a clearly defined chain of command for eventual implementation of those solutions.

2. Credibility

Credibility is a "perception" issue. If people feel that all constituencies of the parish are responsibly represented among the committee members, then a trust level will be established affirming the mandate for decision making. A committee that is judged to be composed only of "rich people," or only as a group of "Father's friends," or only as those who want change at everyone else's expense had best arm itself with crash helmets and combat shields; it will need them!

The importance of responsible representation from all constituencies in most instances will mean extending invitations to membership rather than asking for and accepting all volunteers. The parish council in collaboration with the pastor is an appropriate body for making such recommendations and for extending the invitation to persons active within the community. These persons should be able to articulate the concerns of a particular group while also respecting the needs of others.

Some of the constituencies within a parish might include:

- the "old timers," perhaps even "founders" of the parish
- families with children
- "conservatives"
- "progressives"
- ethnic minorities
- people with different levels of income

Additional concerns would be represented by:

- musicians
- those involved in the ongoing formation of candidates for Christian initiation
- members of the liturgy committee
- members of the finance board

How large should this committee be? Twenty people (with a balance of men and women) is probably the limit. More than twenty becomes unwieldy. Allowing for a few absences at each meeting, a maximum of twenty insures a reasonable number of people present for deliberation and decision making. Twelve to eighteen people is ideal.

B. The Development (or Refinement) of a Parish Mission Statement

The mission statement defines the parish's sense of identity, articulates its vision for the future, and indicates its priorities. This statement should be brief and compact, easily grasped, and used as the basis for all decisions affecting the parish. If the parish already has a mission statement, it should be reviewed to see whether it adequately and truthfully describes the parish's reality and whether the proposed building project is embraced by it. This mission statement is an important foundation for justifying the implementation of the project as well as assisting in the fund-raising phase.

Parish mission statements answer questions such as:

Who is the parish?
What is the parish's purpose?
What are the parish's goals?
How does the parish hope to implement its goals?
What does the parish believe?
How does the parish see itself called to grow and mature?

An example of a brief mission statement is as follows:

St. _____ Parish is a community of Christians responding to the call of Jesus under the guidance of the Holy Spirit, who, associated with other parishes in the Archdiocese and served by pastoral and representative leadership, strive to serve the world by mutual assistance in Christian life, witness, service and worship, and to prepare the Kingdom of God as proclaimed in the Scriptures.

Bishop Thomas J. Gumbleton, D.D.
Archdiocese of Detroit[1]

The mission statment for St. Pius V Catholic Community in Pasadena, Texas, represents a more expansive version of a parish mission statement:

Parish Mission Statement
St. Pius V
Catholic Community

We, the Catholic community of St. Pius V, long established in the Pasadena area, are a multi-ethnic people, located within the Diocese of Galveston-Houston. We are closely bound to our diocesan family and the universal Roman Catholic Church.

Ours is a culturally diverse community, ecumenical in focus, striving to serve all who come to us. As God's co-workers, be-

---

[1] William J. Rademacher, *The Practical Guide for Parish Councils* (West Mystic, CT: Twenty-Third Publications, 1980) 177.

15

lieving in Jesus Christ and His teachings, we are called to mature in our faith, hope and love so that we may share with others the joy He promises.

Our beliefs are . . .

Jesus is alive and active in us, and we are ever renewed in His Spirit through His covenant Love.

He entrusts us to be stewards of His creation.

We are a visible sign of Christ's presence and by His Grace, companions along the pathway leading to God.

Providing justice and upholding dignity for all people is a way of seeing Jesus Christ in others.

As a Catholic community we are called to . . .

Nurture the spiritual life and growth of our community and our Church.

Preach the Good News of God's Kingdom as it is now and in the world to come.

Evangelize by spreading the Good News through word and example, especially as it manifests itself in human justice, peace, dignity and a wholesome environment.

Minister to the needs of all, from the unborn to the elderly, and in turn, be ministered to by all, especially as they exhibit particular pain or problems.

Give due consideration to the world-wide issues being deliberated by our Bishops, and be supportive of their resolves.

C. The Assessment of Parish Physical Resources— Buildings and Grounds in Light of the Mission Statement

The vision expressed by the mission statement will help broaden the perspective of how the new or renovated worship space relates to the entire site owned by the parish and how it should interact with the existing structures or circumstances. Priorities given in the statement concerning the celebration of liturgy, the social interaction of parishioners, and relationship to the neighborhood and world beyond the Church will make different demands for design solutions than simply orientation to parking lots. Existing buildings should be looked at for their state of repair, their adequacy for the needs they fill, their use (or usefulness!) in light of the mission statement.

D. Assessment of Financial Capabilities

Potential resources available for the proposed project must be realistically considered. Some of the information helpful for this assessment would include:

- the stability of present income. What is the annual income? Does the parish depend on annual fund-raiser events (such as a fair or raffle) or regular events such as bingo games to cover ordinary operating expenses? Is there an annual increase in parish income? By what percentage? To what do you attribute the increase?
- a study of economic demographics of parishioners as a whole, and their possible capability of additional contributions for a capital-outlay campaign. What is the range of incomes within the parish? How many parishioners fit within the highest level, the lowest, and a middle range? What are the average contributions within each income level? What percentage of income does the average contribution within each level represent?
- might the parish consider a tithing program instead of a capital outlay fund drive? If the parish already has a tithing program, would it make sense to consider increasing the tithing amount to cover the building costs as well as long-term funding of increased programming and services once the project is completed?
- a study of demographics of the geographical area or region. Is the area growing? If so, by what percentage? Is the local economy growing? By what percentage? (This information is available from municipal or regional civic sources.) By extrapolation, what are the implications or projections for continued growth and the financial stability of the parish?

2 Selection of a Liturgical Consultant

A. Do We Need One?

Relying on the principles in the Constitution on the Sacred Liturgy (1963) and in the *General Instruction of the Roman Missal* (1969), the United States bishops' document EACW emphasizes the importance of a liturgical consultant when it says in paragraph 44:

> Whether designing a new space for the liturgical action or renovating an old one, teamwork and preparation by the congregation (particularly its liturgy committee), clergy, architect and consultant (liturgy and art) are essential. A competent architect should have the assistance of a consultant in liturgy and art both in the discussion stages of the project (dialogue with congregation and clergy as well as among themselves) and throughout the stages of design and building.

Although EACW was published in 1978, and much discussion has ensued since then concerning the definition of the role of the liturgical consultant, the bottom line remains that church renovation and building projects benefit greatly from the expertise and assistance that these consultants bring to the project. Some dioceses require that projects above a certain cost level include a liturgical consultant, while others include in diocesan building guidelines a strong recommendation for parishes to hire a liturgical consultant.

B. What Does a Liturgical Consultant Do?

A liturgical consultant wears several hats. He or she oversees the dialogue between architect and parish, ensuring that the right questions get asked which will lead to design choices that best serve the worshipping assembly. It is unrealistic to expect that architects be well versed in Church history and ritual, even if they are practicing members of the denomination. Their training does not include such specialized background. Nor does the seminary training of priests or other ministers necessarily prepare them for the range of considerations which will most help a community that is building or renovating a place for worship. The liturgical consultant offers the parish expertise in art and architectural history, Church history, the development of sacraments and rites, a knowledge of the intentions and celebration of the rites according to the revised texts, and an understanding of the technical language of both architecture and liturgy. Such a person becomes a ''pathfinder'' through the centuries old thicket of evolving tradition and rites, leading toward new solutions to ancient questions: the same questions asked by every generation of worshippers about what makes an appropriate worship place.

Some of the responsibilities of a liturgical consultant include:

1. assisting in the selection of an architect. The liturgical consultant acquaints the planning committee with the guidelines of the American Institute of Architects,[1] explaining standard procedures for identifying potential architects, describing the scope of the project, setting up interviews with architects, and conducting the interviews. The liturgical consultant also identifies for the planning committee the criteria for evaluating the interviews and finally making a selection.

2. helping the parish to become a better client, by enabling the parish to articulate its liturgical and ritual needs to the architect. This responsibility involves a process of reflection by the architect, pastoral staff, building/renovation committee, and the larger parish. This reflection process is essential. It offers the local community the means to articulate its identity and to translate that articulation into tangible materials which not only express and proclaim that identity, but enable the kind of worship that will make the community more of what it already is: the body of Christ.

3. facilitating an educational process that not only will inform the committee and the larger parish, but also initiate a journey of spiritual formation. The completed worship space is to be a tool

[1] See *You and Your Architect*, 1986, The American Institute of Architects, 1735 New York Ave. N.W., Washington, DC 20006.

in an ongoing formation experience, not an end in itself. The liturgical consultant helps the parish employ the construction project as an opportunity to generate the building up of the community and the renewal of its common life. This can occur in a variety of ways to be discussed below in chapter 4.

4. critiquing, from a liturgical perspective, the architectural designs in the schematic and construction documents phases of the project. Once the committee has arrived at a consensus concerning the conceptual direction desired for the architectural plans, the liturgical consultant helps the committee evaluate whether or not the architect's proposals meet those expectations. The liturgical consultant, in dialogue with the architect, monitors the progress of the designs, keeping alert to the development of anything that might inadvertently impede the stated intentions.

5. advising the planning committee concerning the most effective conceptual design of ritual objects. These include: the baptismal font, altar, ambo, cross, tabernacle, processional cross, vessels and display of the sacred oils, candleholders and stands, devotional images, stained glass images, stations of the cross, festival hangings or processional items, and vesture.

6. helping to identify artists for commissions, assisting in the dialogue with artists, and negotiating contracts with them. The liturgical consultant also works with artists to help them understand the conceptual basis for the work commissioned and critiques the design proposals.

7. assists with the planning of a "leave-taking" ritual in a renovation project and the Rite of Dedication for the completed worship space.

C. Where Do We Find a Liturgical Consultant?

Finding a liturgical consultant is possible; it is not easy. There are not yet enough of them conveniently located across the country, although this is fortunately beginning to change. The Office of Divine Worship of the Archdiocese of Chicago and Catholic Theological Union in Chicago have inaugurated the Institute for Liturgical Consultants in an effort to prepare more people for this profession.[2] Lay and clergy participants in the Institute come from all parts of the

---

[2] For further information on this program, write to: The Institute for Liturgical Consultants, Catholic Theological Union, 5401 S. Cornell Ave., Chicago, IL 60615.

country with diverse backgrounds in art, architecture, liturgy, theology, and pastoral experience. They are the foundation for a new generation of consultants, following the "grandparents" of the movement, active for the most part beginning from the early 1960s, and their handful of descendants of the 1970s and 1980s. There are several good sources for identifying liturgical consultants:

1. The Federation of Diocesan Liturgical Commissions (FDLC) in Washington, DC, publishes a national directory of consultants, *Liturgical Consultants for Worship Space*.[3] It includes names, addresses, and information about their experience, services, and qualifications. Inclusion in this directory is based on recommendation from the regional Roman Catholic diocesan liturgy commissions.

2. Some regional diocesan liturgy commissions have begun to compile their own informal lists or directories of liturgical consultants, architects, and artists.[4] Direct inquiry to the regional diocesan liturgy commission or office of worship may provide more up-to-date information on qualified candidates in the immediate area. Staff people in these offices are often acquainted with others in nearby states who could also make recommendations. There is considerable "networking" among offices of worship and liturgical commissions.

3. Contact parishes that have completed building projects in conjunction with a liturgical consultant. Find out who served as consultant on the project and talk with the people involved about their experience with that consultant.

4. Attend national and regional conferences such as Form/Reform[5] or IFRAA (Interfaith Forum on Religion, Art and Architecture).[6]

[3] This directory is available from The Federation of Diocesan Liturgical Commissions, P.O. Box 29039, Washington, DC 20017.

[4] Examples include: The Office of Liturgy, Diocese of San Diego, 1659 Santa Paula Dr., San Diego, CA 92111-6898; The Office of Worship, Diocese of Galveston-Houston, 1700 San Jacinto St., Houston, TX 77002; The Office of Divine Worship, Archdiocese of Chicago, 1800 N. Hermitage Ave., Chicago, IL 60622-1101.

[5] For information about the Form/Reform conferences, write: Form/Reform, The Conference on Environment and Art for Catholic Worship, Conference Coordinator, P.O. Box 5226, Rockford, IL 61125.

[6] For information about IFRAA conferences and publications, write: Interfaith Forum on Religion, Art and Architecture, 1777 Church St. N.W., Washington, DC 20036.

Diocesan workshops and seminars also provide opportunities to see presentations of work and to meet consultants.

D. How Do We Interview Liturgical Consultants?

Having identified potential liturgical consultants, the next step is to write or telephone those persons, giving a brief description of what you initially see as the scope of the project, and inquiring whether they are interested in being interviewed as a liturgical consultant for the project. If they are interested, ask them for a résumé, and invite them for an interview at a mutually agreeable time. Be prepared to pay the consultant's travel and overnight expenses if distance requires it.

The interview for each candidate should be attended by all the members of the planning committee, pastor, and staff personnel involved in the project. If possible, several candidates should be interviewed so that the committee can experience different approaches among consultants who may bring a variety of backgrounds to the profession. Guidelines for interviewing consultants might include questions about the following topics:

1. Description of qualifications
2. Experience
3. Slides, videotape, or photographs of work
4. Description of services the consultant would provide
5. Description of the kind of educational process the consultant is prepared to offer the planning committee and larger parish
6. The consultant's availability to work on your project within your time schedule
7. Description of the consultant's business structure. Is the consultant associated with a firm which sells church furniture and supplies? Or a firm which employs its own artists to fabricate the appointments for churches? If so, would the consultant expect that all furniture, appointments, and art works would be provided by his or her firm?
8. Names of previous clients and architects with whom consultant has worked who are willing to serve as references
9. Description of fee schedule

All of these topics are of a rather factual, objective nature. There is another level of perception, however, to which the committee should be attentive during the interview, as well as in conversations with the consultant's references. This is a more subjective intuition. For example, does the consultant come with preconceived notions of what you ought to do? Does the consultant have a "package" that he or she more or less imposes on each project? Or do you get the impression that the consultant sees each project as different and will journey with you in exploring the unique story of your parish which will affect your final design responses? Do you feel that the consultant has respect for you? Is he or she condescending? Is this person articulate? Do you think this person would be a good teacher and facilitator for the larger parish? Are you comfortable with this person? You will spend a great deal of time over the next months with the consultant. It is important to choose someone who will help make your project a positive experience for all concerned.

E. How Much Will the Services of a Liturgical Consultant Cost?

Fee arrangements vary among liturgical consultants. Typical methods of determining fees include (1) a fixed rate for agreed upon services, with the number of meetings and details of the process specified, (2) hourly rates, (3) fees based upon a percentage of the project cost, and (4) combinations of these options.

A fixed rate might fit an instance in which the parish contracts for a specified number of meetings with the parish, architect, and planning committee at a per diem rate. Fees range between several hundred to several thousand dollars per day, depending upon the experience and reputation of the consultant and the extent of services provided.

Prevailing hourly rates in 1994 fall between $75 and $150.

Some consultants determine fees using a sliding scale depending upon the complexity and total cost of the project. Projects under $500,000 may be negotiated at a higher percentage fee than those over that amount. Alternatively, on large budget, multi-million dollar projects whose scope is not certain at the outset, the consultant may charge 1.5–2 percent or more, with an agreed upon cap beyond which compensation will not extend.

A combination of options might include a separate contract for a parish educational process negotiated on an hourly or per diem basis, while the work with the architect and planning committee through programming, schematic design, design development, and construction phases might be based on a percentage of project costs.

Ask the consultant to submit a compensation proposal based on the services agreed upon. Travel expenses are usually in addition to the consulting fees and are billed as they occur. There may be additional expenses for telephone and fax charges, and other incidentals as agreed upon between the client and the consultant.

3 Selection of an Architect

Choosing an architect is the next step after selecting a liturgical consultant, and it is accomplished in a similar fashion. Candidates are identified, contacted, interviews set up, and each candidate given an opportunity to make a presentation to the planning committee.

The planning committee first composes a prospectus letter indicating that it is seeking professional architectural services. The letter should describe the scope of the project as presently understood. The letter should include the type of facility desired (such as a church for eight hundred people with social hall and office spaces), whether the project is new construction or a renovation job (or a combination of both), site location, and approximate budget. This letter is then sent to the individuals or firms which the committee is interested in interviewing, asking that they call or write if they wish to be considered.

A. How Do We Find Architects Who Might Be Interested in Our Project?

Start with personal experience to find potential architects for the project. Are there members of the committee who have worked with firms in the city or region? What are their recommendations? Have other worship facilities been built or renovated recently in the area? Find out who the architects were and talk to the owners about their experience with the architects. Are there new or newly renovated buildings in the area, whether they are churches or not, that impress you? A new city library or hotel might be an insightful indication of how an architect works with public spaces.

In addition to these possibilities for identifying architects, it is possible that the diocesan worship office has a list of architects who have worked on churches and with whom the diocesan authorities have had good experiences.

There is also the possibility that the congregation includes one or more architects who want to be considered for the job. If a member of the parish is considered, that person should be interviewed along with other candidates. Parishioners may or may not be the best qualified professionals for the project. From the outset it should be clear, if parishioners are considered, that compensation is negotiated on a professional scale. Parishioner candidates should not be pressured to feel that they can get the job if their fees are less than competitors' fees. Nor is it fair to assume that parishioner candidates *should* be willing to work for less. They should be considered competitively.

The prospectus letter is then sent to the identified architects. It is possible that not all the firms will be interested in your project. Some may not work on churches at all. Some may be too busy to take on a project. Send out enough letters to insure that the response provides a minimum of three to five firms to interview. Talking with that minimum number will indicate architects' different styles of working with clients and enable the committee to make a real choice. Six to eight interviews should probably be the outermost limit for scheduling.

B. Setting Up the Interviews

The most efficient way to interview architects is to allot each the same amount of time, say 30–45 minutes, and schedule them consecutively at one sitting if possible. When scheduling, ask the candidates if they need projection facilities, easels for displaying boards, or VCR equipment. If projection equipment will be used, it is important to schedule interviews in a room capable of being darkened. Allow time for breaks and "turn around" for one candidate to leave and the next to arrive and set up.

By scheduling the interviews for one session, the committee will have all the data and impressions at one time, with everyone having heard all the candidates. They can "debrief" afterward and, with their impressions still fresh, at least tentatively prioritize their preferences based on what they have seen and heard.

C. What Are the Principles for Interviewing Architects?

In an interview the planning committee is interviewing the architect, but the architect is also interviewing you. The American Institute of Architects (AIA), in their guidelines for architects, describes interviews as "exercises in human relations." They say ". . . the purpose of the interview is to show the client that their working relationship will be an interesting and rewarding experience." Knowing that the architect will attempt to present the firm positively and to encourage the exchange of ideas that will indicate what it would be like working together helps the planning committee to anticipate what the meeting will be like.

The AIA suggests that the architect's presentation in an interview include the general background of the firm, its experience, especially with projects similar to yours, information about how they would staff the project, and their record of cost and scheduling performance.

It is inappropriate for two good reasons to expect the architect to present plans or sketches of proposals for the project at an interview. First, the whole purpose of the "programming" phase of working with the architect is to determine exactly the needs that must be addressed in the design solutions. The architect cannot provide solutions for requirements that have not yet been articulated. The description of those requirements will only come after reflection on all the issues together with the liturgical consultant and planning committee. Second, it costs the firm considerable money in time and research to provide what are useless designs if they are not selected for the job and what will probably be useless designs if they *are* selected for the job. You are hiring an architect to work with you on your project, not to arrive with a plan for what you should do.

Here are some questions that may help facilitate conversation with the candidates during the interview:

- Is the architect willing to work with a liturgical consultant?
- Will the architect give your job his or her personal attention from beginning to end, or will someone else handle the job?
- How often will the architect visit the building site when under construction?
- What services are *not* included in the architect's fee? For example, are models included?
- Which of his or her previous projects does the architect consider the most successful? Why?

- Why would the architect like to work on this project? What challenges does this project provide the architect?

D. How Do We Make a Choice of the Candidates We Have Interviewed?

At the end of the several consecutive interviews, the interview committee should poll itself for impressions that lead to an initial prioritizing of the candidates. The next step is to contact references submitted by the architects, taking the time to discover the experiences of other clients with them. The planning committee might be divided into several smaller groups to undertake this step. In addition, committee members may wish to visit buildings designed by the candidates and look at the buildings themselves for impressions. After all this legwork is completed, the committee then meets again, presents the findings of the smaller groups to the whole, and then looks at how the additional information affects their initial list of preferences.

If a first choice is not yet clear, the committee may wish to meet again with representatives of the firms that seem equal contenders. Visiting the architects in their offices, seeing them at work, and getting a sense of the atmosphere of their working environment may help with the choice.

If a first choice does become clear at this point, it is appropriate to so notify that firm and set up a meeting to discuss services and compensation. The unsuccessful candidates should also be notified that a choice has been made, thanking them for their interest and participation in the interviews.

E. What is Involved in Identifying the Architectural Services We Need?

The architect the committee has chosen in all likelihood will talk with you about services as described in the AIA's document called the "Schedule of Designated Services."[1] This document is reproduced

[1] *You and Your Architect* (Washington: The American Institute of Architects, 1986). For a detailed description and discussion of the content of the "Schedule of Designated Services," see AIA Document B163 (David Haviland, ed., *The Documents, The Architects Handbook of Professional Practice,* American Institute of Architects, 1735 New York Ave. N.W., Washington, DC 20006) 1993.

as Figure 1. This chart summarizes the array of services offered by architects. Even small projects can be complex, and it is important to understand the sequence of things that typically happen in an architectural project.

The standard services common to almost all projects are described as the "Basic Services" in the *Standard Form of Agreement Between Owner and Architect*, AIA Document B141, which your architect will probably use for the contract with you. These basic services include:

1. *Schematic Design Phase.* This would cover everything from assessing all the information provided the architect in terms of its design implications and creating a design in response to that information, to estimating probable structural, mechanical, electrical and civil engineering needs, and providing an initial "ballpark" estimate of costs.
2. *Design Development Phase.* After approval of the schematic designs, the architect refines all of the categories initially described in the schematic designs, specifying materials choices and providing a more detailed estimate of costs.
3. *Preparation of Construction Documents.* This means the drawing of all the details of the project for the contractors to use for the actual construction.
4. *Contract Bidding.* At this point the architect checks all the documents, making sure all approvals have been obtained, sending the construction drawings out for bid, evaluating the bids, and negotiating the construction agreements.
5. *Construction.* The architect is responsible for overseeing the on-site construction process and seeing the project to its completion.

In addition to the "Basic Services" described above, the committee may also need services described in the "Schedule of Designated Services" as "Predesign Services" and "Site Development Services." Predesign services include such items as programming (determining needs), surveys of existing facilities, economic feasibility studies, project development scheduling, and project budgeting. Site development services would include site selection (if the site is not already owned), site planning, utilities analyses, environmental studies, and zoning processing assistance. There are also post-contract and supplemental services which are client options enumerated in lines .49–.83 on the chart.

It is the responsibility of the planning committee to confer with the architect concerning the range of services to be contracted. It is possible that some of the services, particularly those covered under

ARTICLE 1.1: SCHEDULE OF DESIGNATED SERVICES

PROJECT:

PROJECT #:

DATE:

Phases:
1 — Pre-Design Phase
2 — Site Analysis Phase
3 — Schematic Design Phase
4 — Design Development Phase
5 — Contract Documents Phase
6 — Bidding or Negotiations Phase
7 — Contract Administration Phase
8 — Post-Contract Phase

*R: RESPONSIBILITY   **M: METHOD OF COMPENSATION

	1 R/M	2 R/M	3 R/M	4 R/M	5 R/M	6 R/M	7 R/M	8 R/M	Remarks and Exceptions
Project Admin. & Mgmt. Services									
.01 Project Administration									
.02 Disciplines Coordination/Document Checking									
.03 Agency Consulting/Review/Approval									
.04 Owner-Supplied Data Coordination									
.05 Schedule Development/Monitoring									
.06 Preliminary Estimate of Cost of the Work									
.07 Presentation									
Pre-Design Services									
.08 Programming									
.09 Space Schematics/Flow Diagrams									
.10 Existing Facilities Surveys									
.11 Marketing Studies									
.12 Economic Feasibility Studies									
.13 Project Financing									
Site Development Services									
.14 Site Analysis and Selection									
.15 Site Development Planning									
.16 Detailed Site Utilization Studies									
.17 On-Site Utility Studies									
.18 Off-Site Utility Studies									
.19 Environmental Studies and Reports									
.20 Zoning Processing Assistance									
.21 Geotechnical Engineering									
.22 Site Surveying									
Design Services									
.23 Architectural Design/Documentation									
.24 Structural Design/Documentation									
.25 Mechanical Design/Documentation									
.26 Electrical Design/Documentation									
.27 Civil Design/Documentation									
.28 Landscape Design/Documentation									
.29 Interior Design/Documentation									
.30 Special Design/Documentation									
.31 Materials Research/Specifications									
Bidding or Negotiation Services									
.32 Bidding Materials									
.33 Addenda									
.34 Bidding/Negotiation									
.35 Analysis of Alternates/Substitutions									
.36 Special Bidding									
.37 Bid Evaluation									
.38 Contract Award									
Contract Administration Services									
.39 Submittal Services									
.40 Observation Services									
.41 Project Representation									
.42 Testing and Inspection Administration									
.43 Supplemental Documentation									
.44 Quotation Requests/Change Orders									
.45 Contract Cost Accounting									
.46 FF&E Installation Administration									
.47 Interpretations and Decisions									
.48 Project Closeout									
Post-Contract Services									
.49 Maintenance and Operational Programming									
.50 Start-Up Assistance									
.51 Record Drawing									
.52 Warranty Review									
.53 Post-Contract Evaluation									

Figure 1. [AIA Schedule of Designated Services]

ARTICLE 1.1: SCHEDULE OF DESIGNATED SERVICES (continued)

PROJECT:

Supplemental Services

PROJECT #:

DATE:

9

*R: RESPONSIBILITY **M: METHOD OF COMPENSATION	R	M	Remarks and Exceptions
.54 Special Studies			
.55 Tenant-Related Services			
.56 Special Furnishings Design			
.57 FF&E Services			
.58 Special Disciplines Consultation			
.59 Special Building Type Consultation			
.60 Fine Arts and Crafts			
.61 Graphic Design			
.62 Renderings			
.63 Model Construction			
.64 Still Photography			
.65 Motion Picture and Videotape			
.66 Life Cycle Cost Analysis			
.67 Value Analysis			
.68 Energy Studies			
.69 Quantity Surveys			
.70 Detailed Cost Estimating			
.71 Environmental Monitoring			
.72 Expert Witness			
.73 Materials and Systems Testing			
.74 Demolition Services			
.75 Mock-Up Services			
.76 Coordination of Designated Services			
.77 FF&E Purchasing/Installation			
.78 Computer Applications			
.79 Project Promotion/Public Relations			
.80 Leasing Brochures			
.81 Pre-Contract Administration/Management			
.82 Extended Bidding			
.83 Extended Contract Administration/Management			

Supplemental Services

Other Services

*R: RESPONSIBILITY
A Architect
O Owner
N Not Provided

**M: METHOD OF COMPENSATION
1. Multiple of Direct Personnel Expense
2. Professional Fee Plus Expenses
3. Percentage of Construction Cost
4. Stipulated Sum
5. Hourly Billing Rates
6. Multiple of Amounts Billed to Architect
7. Other: _____

In conjunction with the descriptions of terms and conditions of this Agreement, the Designated Services, where identified above by appropriate initial, shall be provided by the Owner or the Architect or not at all. In conjunction with the compensation and payment terms of this Agreement, the Owner shall compensate the Architect for such designated services performed by the Architect on the basis of the Method of Compensation identified above by an appropriately keyed number.

KEY

☐ All services performed in normal chronological order.

▨ Services performed out of normal sequence, or not typically provided during these phases, as in FAST-TRACK construction. Such services may warrant special requirements as to responsibility and/or compensation.

OWNER _____
(Signature)

ARCHITECT _____
(Signature)

4 B163—1993

site analysis, might be provided by parishioners with such expertise and professional capabilities. Having decided on the services needed, the next step is to agree on compensation for the architect.

F. How Much Will Architectural Services Cost?

It is best to begin with the architect's submission of a compensation proposal based on the scope of services agreed upon. Typical methods of compensation include a stipulated sum for the whole project, a percentage of the construction cost, hourly rates, or combinations of these. Initially the contract may only be for preliminary services and master planning at an hourly rate. Hourly rates will include a scale of fees beginning with the lowest for apprentice drafting assistants to the highest for principals in the firm. The subsequent services, beginning with the Schematic Design phase, might then be based on a percentage rate of construction cost or a stipulated sum.

Percentage fees will vary regionally. Large metropolitan areas command higher fees than smaller towns. The east and west coasts as well as resort/vacation areas usually are more expensive than elsewhere. The scale of the project and the projected budget are variables that affect percentage fees. Multi-million dollar complexes will often be negotiated at a lower rate than smaller projects. Some dioceses have established caps for architectural service percentage fees. A diocesan cap unrealistically lower than prevailing scales in the region may limit a church client's choices of architectural firms. At present percentage fees range from 7.5–10 percent and more. The architect will assess for the committee the best way of determining fees for the project.

There will also be costs not included in the architect's fees, such as reimbursable costs (travel expenses, reproduction of contract documents, telephone and fax expenses), or costs for site surveys, soils-engineering services, technical tests during construction, fees for outside consultants, and so forth. These expenses, normally billed as they occur, will be detailed as owner responsibilities in the *Owner-Architect Agreement*.

4 Getting Down to Work

The planning committee has been formed and the liturgical consultant and architect are on board. Together they now proceed through a six-phase process in which the liturgical consultant's role is to shape the discussion and facilitate discernment, within a progression of stages structured by the architectural schedule. The phases of the planning process are:

1. Pre-design and programming
2. Master site plan
3. Schematic design
4. Design development
5. Preparation of construction documents, bidding, construction
6. Post-construction education and reflection on use of new worship space

Each of these phases will be discussed, considering the goals and the nature of the work with the architect, planning committee, and the assembly. The investment of time and energy by the planning committee and assembly varies according to the phase.

A. Pre-Design and Programming

Goal: The purpose of the pre-design and programming phase is to collect information and to generate conceptual ideas concerning the ritual requirements of the worship space. During this time an intense liturgical fomation of the architect and committee occurs within their meetings, as well as a parallel formation of the larger assembly. NO DRAWINGS ARE CONCEIVED AT THIS STAGE.

1. Work with the Architect

This pre-design time is a very busy one for the architect. If the project includes a master site plan, the architect will survey existing facilities and ask for information from the client. Architects usually provide an information request form of one or more pages to be completed for every existing as well as anticipated new space. The information requested includes description of use (such as a classroom, small-group discussion area, informal social space, kitchen, or chapel), how many people it must accommodate, whether it is planned for use by children or adults, the frequency of use, and special furniture, equipment, or storage needs. This information should reflect not just the present situation but anticipated needs as well.

The best way to obtain this information is to poll the people most involved in each area or activity. In this way a large number of parishioners are immediately brought into the planning process, promoting ownership of the project.

An efficient way to gather the information is to convene temporary advisory committees, assigning each to study an area or an activity. A key person might be invited to chair each group, with the charge to invite others or ask for volunteers to join the committee.

Depending on the project, various advisory committees might address needs of:

- parking
- nursery
- religious education
- youth ministry
- RCIA
- sacristans
- ushers
- art and decor
- music
- office staff
- social activities
- fair organizers
- clothes closet for the poor
- food pantry for the poor
- school

In addition to gathering the data described above for master planning purposes, the architect should be present for the liturgical consultant's work with the planning committee in reflecting on the community's worship needs. These insights will have important consequences for the architect's master planning as well as specific consequences for the worship space.

2. Work with the Planning Committee

The work of the planning committee during the programming stage is two-fold: to coordinate the advisory committees and to come to a consensus about conceptual principles in dialogue with the liturgical consultant. The coordinating of the advisory committees is a matter of logistics. It entails appointing the chairpersons of the groups, communicating to them the instructions for inviting participation and collecting the needed information, and finally determining how the information will be presented to the architect. The latter may take the form of written summaries and include further conversations with the groups at a later time, or perhaps it will involve presentations made to the planning committee by the chairperson so that all the members of the committee have a sense of the vision expressed by the groups.

The more involved work of the planning committee is to reflect upon all the liturgical issues which bear upon design solutions. This is likely to require a series of meetings extending over a number of months. In preparation for these discussions, the members of the committee should be familiar with EACW. The committee will also find helpful my book *Shaping a House for the Church*.[1] The guidelines developed in EACW provide the foundation for my book as well as the general principles to be discussed below.

a. HOSPITALITY OF SITE

According to EACW, hospitality is an essential part of Christian identity, for the community's hospitality as the body of Christ is the hospitality of Christ. For this reason the committee must carefully consider the initial image of the site and building project. Does the community's mission statement refer to reaching out beyond itself? If so, how does the site express this? Does the building simply face the street or highway with a facade to impress passers-by, or do the design of the site and placement of the building make all people feel welcome to enter and explore what may lie beyond the

[1] Marchita Mauck, *Shaping a House for the Church* (Chicago: Liturgy Training Publications, 1990).

entrance? Does the idea for the site imply that only certain kinds of people would be welcome here? Is there an urge for the church to be walled or fenced off from the rest of the world, for it to be a *sanctuary from* rather than a *presence in* the world?

In addition to the over-all impression of welcome that one perceives at first approach, is the site designed so that there is a clear sense of direction? Is it visually apparent where one enters? Can one distinguish the entry to the church from entry to other buildings on the site? If the church is part of a larger complex, is it apparent that all the parts of the complex are related to the church as the central place which gives meaning to and animates all the rest? Is there a natural flow from the church to the other areas which invites movement back and forth? Such an invitation to move back and forth is part of the formation of the community. It is a rehearsing, so to speak, of the Christian mission of celebrated faith leading to action and participation beyond the ritual events, and then bringing the assembly back to the ritual place for the nourishment that will send them forth again.

Is the sense of direction more than efficient vehicular and pedestrian traffic patterns? Does movement through the interior and exterior spaces honor human needs for beauty, for visual focal points that beckon from one place to another, for order, for safety, for a sense of well-being?

b. PORTAL/ENTRY/THRESHOLD

The physical entrance into the church marks a significant boundary. It is a demarcation between "this side" and the "other side." To cross the threshold and arrive on the "other side" is a body language gesture of willingness to enter into the life on the other side; that is, to enter willingly into the life of the Christian community beyond the portal. Because the Christian community asks the faithful to make a fundamental death and life decision, to embrace the death of Christ in baptism in order to enjoy the grace of new life both now and forever, it is very important that our entry express the seriousness and awe with which we respond to God's invitation to enter this place and this new life.

The Rite of Becoming Catechumens acknowledges the symbolic power of crossing the threshold and entering into the faith community's life. The instructions for this rite of acceptance explicitly state the desirability of gathering the assembly, the sponsors, catechists, and presider outside the church. The presider speaks with those to be received concerning their desire for membership in the Church and their willingness to follow Christ. They renounce any non-Christian worship, and their sponsors and the assembly promise to help these people on their journey of faith. Only then does the presider invite the catechumens and the assembly to enter the church. Crossing that threshold is a rite of assent, ritually celebrated because of the enormity of its consequences for the future of each catechumen and the whole assembly. An entrance way indistinguishable from that of the local supermarket cannot possibly honor the importance of the commitment asked of every member of the community each time they enter the church. An entrance way that visibly respects the significance of entry will support the spiritual formation of the community by tangibly expressing the verbal content and intentions of the rites.

C. BAPTISM

There are several issues to be considered in providing the community an appropriate ritual place for baptism. The baptismal font simply but eloquently invites us into the mystery it bears (fig. 2). In its ample and dark waters people become new creations. Without the encounter with death, in fact the vanquishing of death in the waters of death, there is no Church. God acts in those waters, washing away sin and destruction, infusing new life with the breath of the Spirit, lifting one into the new creation, into God's own life and God's own future. The assembly stands in awe before the stirring of the water at its blessing and the plunging of those being baptized into Christ in the depths of these mighty waters. The embrace of the newborn Christian as he or she is led out of the waters is more than a matter of a towel wrapped around a wet body. It is the Church's joyous embrace of the newborn made palpable for all by the person who took the risk this moment, in this place, to journey triumphantly through the waters of death.

The placement of the font is of critical importance. The Church's own wisdom about the connection of baptism into the community's life and entry into the Church is revealed from the earliest centuries in her placing the baptistery at the entrance to the church (even as a separate building). That original relationship of entry rite and architectural entry was clearly a powerful connection, a resonance of rite and experience that was part of the community's formation.

The modern impulse to place the font "up front" with the altar, ambo, and presider so that all can see sustains a passive attitude

Figure 2. Blessing of the baptismal water. St. Pius V Catholic Church, Pasadena, Texas.

of worship in which the assembly simply watches rites performed before them. Such arrangements make the "sanctuary" a stage rather than a "ritual place." Such a choice deprives the community of its right and responsibility to engage in the rite in a more active way. It deprives the community of a regular encounter with the holy water in the font, not only in the literal touching of the water as one blesses oneself upon entering the church and unleashing the memories associated with being at the font but also in the many other water rites the Church celebrates (such as blessing the deceased at funerals).

Because we are beginning to understand again that it is the Church—not just the priest—which baptizes, it is effective and appropriate that the assembly can actively participate in the initiation rites, particularly at the Easter Vigil. Proximity and active participation in the baptismal rite—rather than passive viewing from afar—underscores the centrality of the assembly's role in the birthing of new members. The assembly participates in the singing of acclamations, in taking the risk of even getting splashed by the baptismal water, in smelling the scented oil poured out in confirmation. The assembly expresses solidarity with the journey of those being in-

Figure 3. Assembly gathered at font for Easter Vigil baptisms. St. Pius V Catholic Church, Pasadena, Texas.

itiated by gathering around the font (fig. 3). This presence confronts the assembly with the necessity of taking up the cross in order to have life. Active participation in the rites of initiation inspires profound recommitment to the journey of Christian life. The font serves best when the assembly can surround it at or near the entry.

The shape of the font contributes to our understanding of the ritual event that occurs in it. Lives are changed as sins are washed away, as death is encountered in the descent into the darkness of the tomb, as the Church gives birth to new members slipping forth from the depths and darkness of the waters into light and life. The early Church used several forms that recall these different experiences of bath, tomb, and womb. Round fonts recalled both bathing and womb imagery. Rectangular shapes suggested tombs, while cruciform fonts reminded the faithful of the cross as image of Christ's passion, death, and resurrection into eternal life. A hexagonal font with its six sides suggested the sixth day (the day of Christ's crucifixion and death), while an octagon's eight sides pointed to the eighth day (the day of the resurrection). Often a hexagonal font was located within an octagonal baptistery to emphasize that the descent into the tomb led to emergence into the new life of the resurrection when the newly baptized person stepped out of the font into the eight-sided room.

Whatever the choice of the shape of the font, the baptismal ritual calls for "living water" rather than still water. The sound of flowing water is appropriate for baptism. Soundless swirling bubblers in shallow pools are more reminiscent of overflowing run-off sewers, hardly an image worthy of the life-giving waters of baptism. Hearing the water before one even sees it invites the worshippers to come to the water for blessing. Hearing the joyous splashes of a font at the beginning of a funeral rite reminds the assembly more powerfully than homiletic words that baptism into the Lord's death is baptism into eternal life in the Lord. The water can cease flowing during the celebration of the Eucharist as the ritual action shifts to the place for proclamation of the Word and table rites. In this way the ritual action takes priority, and the ritual focus determines the role of the ritual object, in this case the flowing water.

The amount of water for baptism is important. Most bluntly stated, there must be enough water to die in! The risk and vulnerability of baptism requires enough water to immerse both infants and adults. There should be at least sixteen or more inches of water, capable of being warmed, in the font.

As the planning committee considers the choices, it is imperative that they ask the questions generated by the above discussion. Is the celebration of the rite the foremost concern for both the placement and the shape of the font? Is the area for baptism (about one-third of the church!) flexible enough so that its power as a rite of passage can be experienced? Does the placement imply that the presence of the assembly is critical because it is the *Church* with Christ presiding that is responsible for the birthing of the neophytes? Does the shape of the font express the ritual actions of "descending into the earth and rising up again," "being born anew," "being washed free from sin" that is all at the heart of holy baptism?

d. RECONCILIATION (PENANCE)

Although the chapel reserved for the celebration of the sacrament of penance is meant for the celebration of the individual rite, its ecclesial symbolism extends to the larger community. A clear spatial relationship with the baptistery enables the reconciliation chapel to recall the connection of penance to baptism, the first experience of the forgiveness of sins. If the location of the reconciliation chapel is related to the font in such a way that the penitent emerges to find himself or herself oriented toward the font, then that person will be drawn to the water, the source of first washing from sin by the Holy Spirit in baptism (fig. 4).

At its most extreme expression reconciliation is a "reentry" rite celebrated after periods of sin, absence, and alienation. The rite reincorporates into the life of the community those who have been separated from it. The Church reaffirms its readiness to build up the community by welcoming back all who surrender to God's mercy and forgiveness and who renew their commitment to participation in the mission of Christ.

The space for the celebration of God's reconciling love is a holy place. It is best seen as a chapel. A tasteful "counseling" room tucked away in some unobtrusive place near the day chapel, or convenient to the sacristy, or backing up to the restrooms is not sufficient. The ritual place requires a sense of solemn expectation— expectation of a transforming encounter with God. This means that the place be reserved only for the celebration of the sacrament of penance. It can not also serve as an ushers' storage room, or a cry room, or a bride's dressing room. The integrity and holiness of the ritual of penance demands an honored place reserved for it alone. The space for reconciliation should also speak of the community's

41

desire for the return of those who are separated. It should honor the vulnerability required for celebrating the sacrament by revealing the sacredness of the invitation. This happens when the space is hospitable, welcoming, and supportive—ample enough to easily accommodate all for face to face confession as well as anonymous participation in the rite, including those in wheelchairs or with walkers.

The planning committee also needs to reflect upon the sacrament of penance as it relates to baptism and the Eucharist. The committee needs to consider how the placement of the chapel expresses the community's hospitality as it offers membership in the community through its entry and reentry rites of baptism, reconciliation and the Eucharist. Where will the reconciliation chapel be located? How will it be oriented to the font? How will it be assured that it is a ritual place made holy by the actions celebrated there?

e. EUCHARIST

Baptism, confirmation, and the Eucharist are the initiatory sacraments of the Church. The Eucharist is the ongoing sacramental celebration that keeps returning us to the implications of life in

Figure 4. Reconciliation chapel located in relationship to baptismal font. St. Pius V Catholic Church, Pasadena, Texas.

Christ. The ritual place for the Eucharist is the space embracing the ambo and altar within the assembly. An elevated platform thrust out into the assembly does not by itself make a ritual place for the Eucharist. If the ambo, altar, and presider's chair (not to mention tabernacle and baptismal font) are all arrayed in a row across this platform, one has a performance stage instead of a ritual place. The place for the Eucharist is not necessarily the "front" of the church. It may be in the center of an assembly gathered around or, given an antiphonal seating arrangement, the Eucharistic space for the altar and ambo may extend along a longitudinal axis between the two halves of the flanking assembly.

Since the entire congregation—the assembly, presider, and other ministers—offers the Eucharist, the altar as central focal point for the rite should be located within the assembly.[2] It should be approachable by the assembly from all sides. A closer view of the action is not the primary reason for locating the place for the Eucharist within the assembly. It is to express an invitation to the gathered people to participate in the giving of thanks that is the Eucharist by fully and consciously offering themselves, their lives, along with the bread and wine as the body of Christ. Since there are occasions when the assembly appropriately encircles the altar, an ample space surrounding the altar anticipates and invites such ritual movement.

Altar platforms anchored to a back wall whose surface design and decoration demand that the wall be seen as a passive "backdrop" for the altar encourage a spectator attitude in the assembly. This wall often becomes an anchor, much larger and more impressive than the altar. When this happens the altar is denied its rightful centrality within the midst of the assembly, and the space cannot properly function as a ritual place. The passive wall takes precedence over active ritual place.

There is an essential relationship between font and table (fig. 5). The ritual spaces for baptism and the Eucharist are meant to be relational. The assembly should first see and then experience the bipolar centrality of baptism and the Eucharist in their life together. The assembly should see and experience that there is a journey to be made between the two. The two ritual centers for baptism and the Eucharist imply movement between the two, a shifting of ritual

---

[2] See the *General Instruction of the Roman Missal*, n. 54, for a discussion of the primary role of the faithful, by virtue of their baptism into the priesthood of Christ, in the offering of the Eucharist.

Figure 5. Ritual spaces for baptismal font and Eucharistic table within the assembly. St. Pius V Catholic Church, Pasadena, Texas.

attention from one place to the other. Thus there really is not a "front" and "back" of the church. When the baptistery is at the entry, then the entry isn't the "back" any more. It is the central focus, the "front" when baptism is celebrated.

It is the responsibility of the planning committee to consider the implications of the celebration of the Eucharist as the culmination of the initiation rites. It is their responsibility to insure that the location of the altar bespeaks a ritual place for all the actions of the Eucharist by the presider, other ministers, and the assembly, and that the design of the Eucharistic ritual place expresses its relationship to the rites of baptism.

A prominent display of the holy oils in beautiful vessels, emphasizing the Church's readiness always to welcome new members and to anoint the sick, is appropriate. Flagons with generous amounts of the holy oils express the hospitality of the baptizing, reconciling community whose worship and life culminate in the thanksgiving of the Eucharist (fig. 6).

f. CONSIDERATION OF OTHER RITES AND
   THEIR RELATIONSHIP TO FONT AND TABLE

The primacy of the ritual places for baptism and the Eucharist within the assembly are incontestable. With places for these sacraments specified clearly within the assembly, the relationship of all the other sacramental rites to them will become clearer. Funerals, weddings, anointing of the sick, and communal penance also need their ritual space, but always within their baptismal and Eucharistic context. It is the inner connectedness between these sacramental rites and their relationship to baptism and the Eucharist that enables them to express their fullness. It is the isolationist treatment given to funerals, weddings, etc. that hinders them from finding their richest expression. The following gives some examples.

i. *Funerals*. Our funeral rites focus on the unity of the deceased with Christ, in particular with the death and resurrection of the Lord. This emphasis is, of course, a baptismal one, because we believe that all who have become one with Christ in baptism will triumph with Christ over death and become one with Christ in eternal life.

At the beginning of the funeral rite, the priest and ministers greet the body at the entry of the church, and the priest blesses the body with holy water reminiscent of the baptismal bath. If this blessing occurs at the baptismal font, the explicit connection of death with Christ in baptism is more obvious. When the white pall is placed

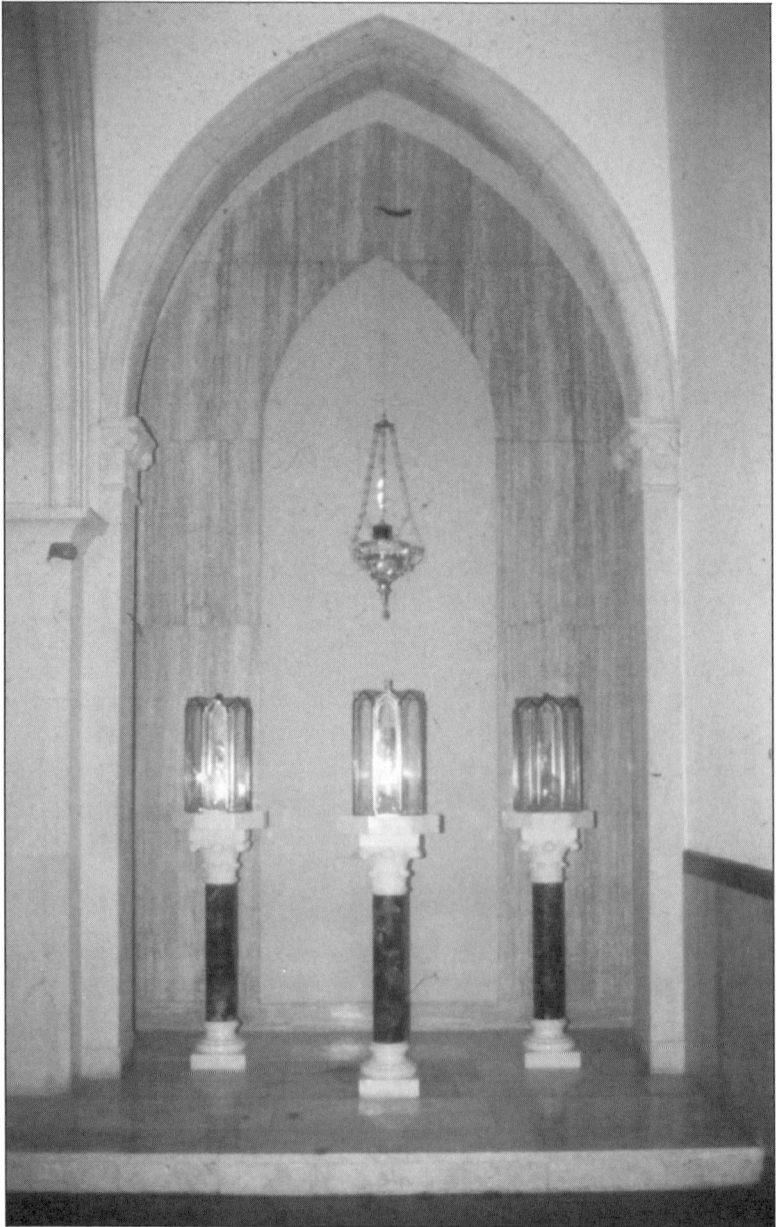

Figure 6. Reservation of Holy Oils. St. Pius V Catholic Church, Pasadena, Texas.

on the casket at the font, the ritual metaphor is the connection with the white baptismal garments. The blessing of the body with baptismal water at the font and the clothing with the white garment become an occasion for the assembly to once more encounter its Christian identity by experiencing the truth of baptismal commitment and baptismal hope in its midst. If the water used for this blessing is water from the sacristy sink, or a small vessel containing water from an unknown source, this gesture can be seen as both minimalist and perfunctory.

The assembly more fully encounters the awesome truth that baptism into Christ's death and resurrection vanquishes death forever when there is space for the casket at the font and for the ministers to approach the font for the opening of the funeral rite. If the gathering space at the font is ample enough, the assembly can gather there for the wake as well (fig. 7). Placing a standing cross near the casket for a wake expresses once more this Christian confidence that in death we are brought home to the cross and to the font, to our entering into Christ's death and resurrection. In doing so the faithful see and experience the implications of their faith in new ways.

Figure 7. Funeral wake with casket at the baptismal font. St. Pius V Catholic Church, Pasadena, Texas.

47

ii. *Weddings.* The sacrament of marriage images for the assembly the unity and love that exists between Christ and his Church. It is the Christian baptism of the bride and groom that renders their marriage sacramental.

An entry location of the font, directly in the midst of the processional path of the bridal couple on their way to the altar where they will exchange their vows, can remind the couple and the assembly of the mystery of love begun in the waters of baptism. Even on this day the bridal couple and the whole assembly must pass by this reminder of being claimed by love incarnate. The couple promises to love each other and be faithful as living examples in the community of Christ's unconditional love and fidelity. As the assembly shifts its focus from the couple's entry into their midst, past the baptismal font, to the ritual place for the Eucharist, the meaning of Christ's sacramental love is recalled and imaged. Dying and rising, being broken and given, is at the core of sacramental love.

iii. *Anointing of the Sick.* The source of the sacrament of anointing is the union of the sick person with the death and resurrection of Christ. The tradition of anointing the sick, recounted in the Letter of James (5:14-16), has as its focus the commendation of the ill to the "suffering and glorified Lord, that he may raise them up and save them." Handing into the Lord's care those who are sick and suffering is to reaffirm with confidence that those who die with Christ will rise with Christ. The baptized are those who have died with Christ in the hope of rising with Christ. The baptized are those who believe that Christ will raise them up and save them.

Given this intimate relationship between baptism as the first sacrament of healing the scars of sin and the sacrament of anointing as the present sacramental experience of Christ's healing and forgiving touch, gathering the sick and their loved ones around the font makes an intentional connection between the ultimate healing baptism offers and the specific grace prayed for in sacramental anointing. If one employs readings that tell of God's mighty deeds of healing with the Spirit, water, oil, and prayer (such as the healing at the pool of Bethsaida [John 5:1f.] or at the pool at Siloam [John 9:1f.]), the assembly's experience at this place will be strengthened. It is these same promises of the forgiveness of sins and the raising up of those who enter into Christ's suffering that are reiterated now in the sacrament of anointing. A procession to the table for the Eucharistic banquet following the Liturgy of the Word and the sacrament of anointing at the font invites the celebration of the Eucharist as grateful praise and thanks for God's mighty acts.

iv. *Penance.* The Church recognizes the ecclesial nature of sin and reconciliation when it points out that the sins of one person always harm others, and the holiness of one always benefits others.[3] The communal rite of penance provides a way of emphasizing the implications of personal sin within the larger community. The alienation and separation of sinners always diminishes the Church, while the reconciliation of sinners builds up the Church and makes it whole. This is visibly evident in communal rites which focus on the need of all for repentance and renewal.

Our first experience of forgiveness of sins is in baptism, the sacrament in which ". . . our fallen nature is crucified with Christ so that the body of sin may be destroyed and we may no longer be slaves to sin, but rise with Christ and live for God."[4] Our ordinary experience of the forgiveness of sins is in the celebration of the Eucharist. There we recall that on the night he was betrayed and began his saving passion, Christ instituted the sacrifice of the new covenant in his blood for the forgiveness of sins.

However, when the assembly gathers for the specific purpose of a communal penance service, the baptismal sources for the sacrament invite reflection on the ways in which those connections might be experienced. Gathering at the font might be a good way to begin. This provides the community the opportunity to revisit the baptismal foundations of reconciliation and to encounter the restorative power of God in Scripture. The assembly's expression of assent to the invitation to together turn back to God might be symbolized by their converging at the font where they consciously ask God's forgiveness. This offers the possibility of reminding them of the ecclesial implications of both sin and conversion, as well as strengthening their awareness of these ritual places as places capable of sustaining a transforming relationship with God.

Another way to celebrate a communal penance rite is to gather at the font at the end of the service following the reading of an appropriate scriptural text, homily, examination of conscience, and a communal expression of sorrow. After the renewal of baptismal vows at the font, the liturgy could close with the assembly's praying the Lord's Prayer around the altar.

[3] Introduction to *The Rite of Penance*, n. 5.
[4] Introduction to *The Rite of Penance*, n. 2.

49

Observation: It should be apparent from the discussion of the anointing of the sick and of penance that the sacraments of initiation (baptism, confirmation, and the Eucharist) are the foundational experience upon which all other sacraments are celebrated. It is in the initiation rites that the ultimate healing and reconciliation of all things in Christ is achieved. Rather than seeing anointing of the sick and reconciliation as unrelated liturgical events disconnected from their baptismal source, I would suggest precisely the opposite. Anointing the sick always has a fuller meaning when situated in a baptismal and Eucharistic context. The sacrament of penance always has a richer foundation when celebrated at or near the place where the believer's sins were originally washed away in baptism. When the community gathers to celebrate the sacraments of the anointing of the sick or penance, emphasizing the relationship of these sacraments to baptism and the Eucharist can only strengthen their integrity and affective power.

g. RESERVED EUCHARIST

Although there is evidence from early times of reserving the Eucharist (but not necessarily within the church, and not visible to the assembly), for about half of our history—the past eight hundred years—the Church has legislated the reservation of the Eucharist. The primary reason for reserving the Eucharist is the Communion of the dying and the sick. In addition, the reserved Eucharist is available to the faithful for private devotion.[5]

Celebration of the Eucharist always takes priority over the reservation of the Eucharist. Thus the place for the active celebration of the Eucharist should take visual and ritual precedence over the location of the tabernacle. This is not to say that the importance of the reserved Eucharist is to be minimized. To the contrary, a beautiful reservation chapel provides both focus and intimacy for private devotion that is not intended within the larger assembly space. A chapel for Eucharistic reservation makes clear the distinction between the *celebration of the Eucharist* and its *reservation.*[6]

The reserved Eucharist is most clearly honored when the tabernacle is the only focal point in the space, effectively lit, and freestanding (fig. 8). When it is on a pillar or in a Eucharistic tower

[5] Introduction to *Holy Communion and Worship of the Eucharist Outside of Mass,* n. 5.
[6] EACW, nn. 78, 80.

50

Figure 8. Pillar tabernacle (with original baptismal font as the base). St. Pius V Catholic Church, Pasadena, Texas.

occupying the center of the space and approachable from all directions, it invites the faithful to encounter the living presence of Christ proclaimed and celebrated in the reserved Eucharist. If the tabernacle is more passively located in a wall niche, care must be taken that the size and proportion and design appropriately honor the reserved Eucharist. The reservation chapel is clearly not intended as a celebration or a public assembly space, but a space of homage, reverence, and awe.

h. DEVOTIONAL IMAGES

i. *Statues of the Saints.* Over the past several centuries devotional images have become primarily pious decoration. Factory-produced painted plaster images of little or no artistic merit "fill in" the high wall spaces between windows or inhabit any available corner. Statues of Mary and Joseph traditionally mark the boundaries of the sanctuary by acting as brackets on the flanking walls. Though looking "churchy," such images decorating the walls above the heads of the faithful contribute little to their real purpose.

Just as the tabernacle in the reservation chapel works more powerfully when it is accessible and barrier free, so also do images of the saints. When they are at eye level, the believer experiences a face-to-face encounter, which demands a different response than when one gazes upwards toward a figure floating against the wall far removed from human life and pain. If the artistic and expressive content of the image engage the believer in a "dialogue" with the work—that is, if the saint's perseverance, weariness, joy, or contentment with his or her life, or courage in the face of adversity speak to the believer—then the "communion of saints" begins to make sense and touch people's lives. They become objects of devotion rather than decoration.

We need more than the demure standing figures holding lilies that are often found in church supply catalogues. Just as in times past, we need our own expressions of the saints in stone, wood, metal, or other materials. The community needs to commission from artists images of feeling and dignity that are capable of bearing the mystery they seek to express. We need to break through the blandness of the visual equivalent of ecclesiastical "elevator music." Instead we need to confront the faithful with the reality of broken lives made new again, of heroic love, of God's profound fidelity and abiding presence with all God's people in all times and places. A change in understanding about what statues of saints are meant to do will occur when the images of the saints inhabit spaces rather than hang on walls. This transformation in perception will occur when the viewers are invited to move around the image, to see it from different angles, and to enter into an experience of the person represented that resonates with their own pains and joys, hopes and aspirations. Designers and planners of worship spaces must consider the human need for encounter and appreciate the priority of quiet spaces for devotional relationship over the display of religious images.

ii. *Stations of the Cross.* Contemporary texts for praying the Stations of the Cross move beyond literal narrative of the passion of Christ to the implications for the believer of "taking up the cross" of Christ. The content of the meditations invites those praying to look into their own lives and to consider the ways in which they enter into Christ's suffering and death, and therefore into Christ's resurrection. Praying this devotion challenges believers to walk with Christ on the route to death in their own lives.

Modern meditations for the Stations of the Cross offer a good model for the visual images. Excessively realistic images deprive the faithful of the challenge to journey with Christ in the present. Dynamic contemporary stations might stimulate the imagination, allowing the viewer to "fill in the gaps" with his or her own experiences of the Cross of Jesus Christ. Perhaps the images would serve better if they raised the social justice consciousness of the participants or enabled them to embrace more fully the paradox of the cross and death for life and meaning. The use of evocative symbols could achieve this more dramatically than mere realistic historical representations.

Placement of the Stations of the Cross determines to a large extent the viewer's participation in the devotion. Grouping all the images together in one place on a wall requires no movement. One can simply sit down and see all of them at once. But the Stations of the Cross are a processional devotion. Not only should the images be placed in a sequence that surrounds the assembly, but a most effective arrangement invites those praying the devotion to walk the course—after all, this is the "way" of the cross. One dramatic way to accomplish the experience of the processional journey is for the stations actually to be embedded in the floor, stepping stones to be followed. Pools of light from above wash over the paving blocks or bronze reliefs, leading one from station to station. A good example of this treatment can be found at the Warren Chapel at the University of Dallas (fig. 9). Here bronze stations are embedded in the floor in a circular concourse surrounding the assembly. People are drawn from one station to the next, not just by the light which bathes each image but also by the very simple and compelling momentum of the images that succeed one upon another. The concourse itself is constructed with paving stones, giving one a sense of making the way of the cross. The "stations," each marked with a Roman numeral, are not so much "pictures" as they are "markers" that remind one of the cost of discipleship and its blessings. Making the Way of the Cross according to this arrangement enables the believer to recall and contemplate particular moments in Jesus' passion while literally walking his journey to glory.

Planners need to ask how one engages the participants in the devotion by the placement of the stations. How do the images impinge on the consciousness and experience of the faithful, leading to action and response in their own lives?

3. Work with the Assembly

At the same time that the architect and planning committee engage in the programming responsibilities of gathering practical data

Figure 9. Eighth Station of the Cross, University of Dallas Chapel, Dallas, Texas. (Liturgical consultant, Lyle Novinsky. Artist, H. Bartscht).

and reflecting upon the liturgical actions that will provide the basis for the design of the worship space, the assembly also has work to do.

a. ADVISORY COMMITTEES

The first contribution that the larger assembly makes is for as many as possible to participate in the work of the advisory committees (see chapter 1). These committees assist in the assessment of existing facilities and compile data requested by the architect. A variety of committees need to look at present facilities and to clarify the practical concerns about those areas and activities that will be affected by the project.

b. THE COMMUNITY'S HISTORY

A major building or renovation project provides the opportunity to reflect upon the community's past as the foundation for its future. It is a wonderful occasion to compile the history of the parish or update it from a previous compilation. This is the time to put out a call for reminiscences about events, personalities, and for old photographs of both the place and events that occurred there. A special social event might be held such as a parish supper, at which the entertainment will be reminiscing about the ups and downs and memorable moments of the church's life. Previous pastors and former parishioners could be invited. Videotaping the ensuing conversation becomes an archival treasure for the next generation. Such a "walk down memory lane" builds community, helps people see anew the journey of faith shared by the members of the community and how their lives and experiences are interdependent. Not least of all, it provides the material for a lively account to be published for the dedication of the completed project.

c. LITURGICAL FORMATION

Bringing the community along through the programming phase is essential for their "ownership" of the project. This means that the whole assembly must be offered the opportunity to grow in their understanding of their worship and to be exposed to the principles and concepts with which the planning committee and architect will be working as the basis for their design proposals.

The strategies for reaching the larger parish include both "informational" outreach efforts in which ideas and concepts are put in the hands of the assembly through printed material and the more interactive opportunities of meetings in which presentations of material and response can occur. Both are important.

i. *Published Materials.* The use of printed material keyed to the progress of the deliberations on specific topics by the planning committee can be very helpful. An example is the series of bulletin inserts on individual topics such as the gathered assembly, the baptismal font, reservation of the Eucharist, and other subjects published by the FDLC in Washington, DC.[7] These inserts can be included in the bulletin over a period of months. In addition, updates on the progress of the planning committee inserted in the bulletin or in letters to parishioners are helpful. Every effort should be made to avoid the perception of ''secret'' deliberations.

ii. *General Parish Meetings.* Beyond the availability of printed explanatory resources, the assembly deserves the opportunity for gathering to reflect upon their worship, what it has been and where it might be headed. Such reflection introduces insights and breaks open new meaning for the assembly as they contemplate a new worship place that will call them to new experiences. Assemblies need reassurance that the past is not being rejected in the act of moving into the future. Change has always been part of the Christian tradition. It is critical to help the assembly see that change is authentic, does not have to be destructive, and can in fact strengthen the values that many feel are most threatened by change.

It is very important that the general parish sessions not be seen as meetings at which a vote will be taken on the direction of the planning or on individual items up for discussion by the planning committee. By giving the committee a mandate to produce a proposal to be submitted to the parish council and pastor, the community has placed its trust in the representatives who make up the committee. The general sessions serve the purpose of bringing to the larger community a reflection process similar to that being experienced by the planning committee. In this way the whole parish is made aware of the important issues and will have background for understanding the proposal which eventually will be presented.

There are several ways in which the general parish sessions might be facilitated. One possibility is the ''town hall'' meeting, a session in which opinions and ideas are expressed without debate or defen-

---

[7] FDLC, the address is noted in footnote 3, chapter 2.

siveness. A workshop format of several hours in an evening or perhaps a Saturday morning could be devoted to presentations of material, accompanied by small-group discussion and reflection. Another option is to schedule a series of retreat days in which prayer and reflection on the issues at hand would be combined in a way that reverently respects the importance of the building project for the whole community. Any of these options might be combined with prayer sessions or social events such as community suppers at which newcomers might be introduced and where all can build relationships with each other.

The previous liturgical experiences of the community, the parish's history, and the assembly's level of awareness of current liturgical and theological insights about worship suggest the style and type of educational experiences to be offered the people. Regardless of the level of sophistication of the community, the community's spiritual as well as financial investment in the new project requires attention in at least three areas: the mission of the community, the larger story of the Church's worship history, and the celebration of sacraments and their implications for the design of worship spaces. At least one and perhaps several general sessions with the whole community should be held for each of these topics.

AA. THE MISSION OF THE COMMUNITY. The mission of the community concerns both its mission statement and its subjective understanding of itself as a people on a journey together in this place at this time. This is an opportunity to remember the parish's story and to recall the changes that have taken place within memory. It is an opportunity to remember apprehensions over past developments and to look back at the changes that occurred twenty or thirty years ago which may have become so familiar that it seems as if things were always as they are now. This is an opportunity for people to express current fears and apprehensions. In the voicing of fears, values can be clarified. The assembly is empowered to claim values when there is the opportunity for shared discussion.

It is important at this meeting for the facilitator to state at the onset that there are no right or wrong feelings when it comes to sharing one's experience. This is a listening session: parishioners listening to each other telling of their experiences in this community. The results are often quite astonishing as the parishioners do for each other what no authority figure or outsider could possibly accomplish. The members demand of each other a balanced view of their own story. The experience of shared past investment in the

57

life of the community becomes the foundation for investing in its future, projecting hopes and aspirations for the nurturing in the faith of generations to come.

BB. THE CHURCH'S WORSHIP HISTORY. Many people simply have no idea of the story of church architecture. They are not aware that the Church's history is quite varied or that the style and arrangement of a church reveals how a community understood itself as a worshipping assembly. Our memories are short, spanning only a couple of generations at most. It is almost always a surprise for people to see the wide range of experiences the Church has had in its long history. To compare the house churches of the third century with the imperial basilicas of Constantine's reign in the fourth century, or those basilicas with Gothic cathedrals, or Gothic cathedrals with Baroque St. Peter's in Rome is to come face to face with the reality of radical change occurring rather regularly in the course of our Church's story. For people to actually see the numerous shifts in the appearance and liturgical function of our churches through the centuries is for them to find reassurance in two facts. First, one authentic part of the Church's tradition is that believers have always shaped buildings to reflect and support their understanding of worship. We have been doing that since the beginning. Second, change is the sign of fidelity to the living faith, of fidelity to the ways in which we are called to be Church in our modern world. To be open to change is paradoxically to be faithful to the most enduring truths of the faith.

A slide presentation of the Christian community's unfolding reflection on its worship as seen in its places of worship over the course of time is a most effective way to remind the community members of our rich heritage. As one looks at the efforts to meet the needs of each succeeding generation, one begins to understand that the questions are not new. Every generation must grapple with the same issues and find its own solutions. Knowing something of the breadth of our tradition enables the present generation to benefit from centuries of wisdom about the same basic questions.

CC. THE CELEBRATION OF SACRAMENTS. This session might be envisioned as a course in the content, intentions, and celebration of sacraments. It would take the cluster of initiation rites (baptism, confirmation, and Eucharist) and look at their implications for the life of the community. Eucharist and baptism would be shown as the matrix for the celebration of the other sacraments. The Rite of Christian Initiation of Adults as a model of the faith journey in the life of the community could be considered. With the goal of spiritual formation of the assembly and growth in the spiritual life together in mind, there could be some reflection on the most effective ways to celebrate the community's rites so that they have the greatest impact on the lives of the assembly. Helping the assembly understand the celebration of the rites as envisioned by the revised texts will prepare the community for the design proposal to be made by the planning committee and will also encourage a more profound entering into those rites.

B. Master Site Plan

Goal: For projects in which a site plan is included, the master site plan phase of the project establishes the location of new construction in relationship to existing structures. The orientation of buildings to each other, to the entire site, and their relationship to the surrounding environment is decided.

1. Architect

The most basic level of site planning includes technical services such as surveying the property, determining the location of utilities, analyzing elevation shifts on the site, and drainage patterns. Existing buildings are blocked in. Then the architect indicates the dimensions of any structural additions for a renovation project, or proposes the location of new construction. Places are indicated on the plan also for any anticipated structures or sites (such as additional parking, recreation areas, ball fields, etc.) that may be constructed as part of long-range plans.

The architect bases the proposals on information gained in the *Pre-Design and Programming* phase described above.

2. Parish Planning Committee

When the architect provides the first design for a master site plan, it is the responsibility of the parish planning committee to look very carefully at the plan in the light of their programming goals. The areas of concern include items such as:

- centrality of worship space as a statement of faith, expessing worship as central to the parish's life. The flow of people to other areas of the complex is important.

59

- relationship of worship space to social areas, office spaces, school or educational facilities
- sense of unity
- hospitality of site
- role of landscape design in supporting programming concepts
- possibilities for exterior ritual spaces, e.g., for gathering the assembly for the Palm Sunday procession into the church, and for the assembly to be present for the lighting of the Easter fire (including exterior electrical jacks for acoustical instruments, mike jacks for proclamation of the Word and music)
- exterior gathering space for the Sunday assembly
- resonance of the plan with the community's mission statement

In discussing the site plan details in light of the programming goals, the plan may be redrawn several times. It is important to think through the implications of the locations of structures and how they relate to each other so that the whole site can best serve the community's worship needs.

3. Assembly

Once the master site plan has been agreed upon, it is appropriate to present the proposal to the larger community. This design is quite schematic. There are as yet no details of the proposed renovation or new building. Only the relationships are established, and relative scales of sites and structures are indicated. At this time the master site plan can be presented in the light of programming goals and the community's mission statement.

C. Schematic Design

Goal: In the schematic design phase the first drawings, based on programming information, are generated.

1. Architect

The architect begins the first drawings of the parts of the master site plan which fall within the scope of the present project. The architect bases these drawings upon the concepts agreed upon in the *Pre-design and Programming* phase, in particular the topics discussed in chapter 4 in "Work with the Planning Committee." In the schematic design phase the architect indicates probable structural, mechanical, electrical, and civil engineering requirements to support the programming goals. By the end of the schematic design phase, it will be possible to project a "ballpark" figure for costs.

2. Parish Planning Committee

This is a rather intense period for the parish planning committee during which it responds to the architect's proposals for achieving the envisioned worship space. The members must be clear and articulate about the concepts they wish expressed in the plans. At this stage the plans are revised a number of times as layouts and relationships are assessed and reworked.

3. Assembly

During this time the assembly does not have a direct role. The committee working on the community's history continues their project.

D. Design Development

Goal: The preliminary designs of the *Schematic Design* phase are refined and finalized.

1. Architect

In the *Design Development* phase the architect works closely with engineering consultants to establish all the specifications for the project. Materials and interior and exterior finishes are decided upon. A more precise estimate of construction costs is provided. Finalized plans are provided, along with a three-dimensional model if this is part of the agreed upon services.

2. Parish Planning Committee

a. The parish planning committee works closely with the architect in the selection of materials and interior and exterior finishes. Final revisions are made to the plans.

b. At this stage the parish planning committee also decides what items will be commissioned from artists. Altar, ambo, tabernacle, paschal candle stand, presider's chair, candle holders, Stations of the Cross, and images of saints are some of the items that might be commissioned. The basic concepts for these will have been considered during the *Pre-design* and *Programming* phase.

i. *Identifying Artists*. The Church has a long tradition of working with artists. It is probable that by commissioning an artist you will acquire more beautiful pieces, of higher quality, designed specifically for your community and site, often at lower prices than you can obtain from religious goods stores or catalogues. There are probably local or regional artists of merit whose work should be considered. Diocesan worship offices can often make recommendations, as can university art departments or other communities who have commissioned works of art. In addition, the newsletter *Environment and Art* regularly showcases the work of artists from throughout the country who are doing good liturgical art.[8]

ii. *Commissioning Work from Artists*. Invite several artists to submit slides of their work (if you are unfamiliar with it). Select those artists whose work interests you the most, and invite them to come for an interview. Select the artist whose work you like the most, and whom you feel is open to working with you in achieving your goal. Explain to the selected artist the concepts behind the commissioned works and ask how he or she might go about meeting the design challenge. Ask the artist to submit to you a proposed fee schedule for designing, and then an estimate for construction and fabrication costs. The artist will then submit a contract for the agreed upon fees as well as agreed upon delivery date.

c. Now that the major decisions about the building have been made and the architect is refining the drawings, the planning committee can turn its attention to considering the environment for worship during the construction of the project. If the community will be worshipping in a temporary space for the duration of the construction, some thought must be given to the arrangement. A temporary space affords the opportunity to begin modeling the seating arrangement and some of the liturgical experiences to be encountered in the new space. To the extent possible, the temporary place for worship should be dignified and beautiful. This is not impossible, even with a small budget. The ideal temporary space will be one which does not have to be dismantled each week.

[8] For subscription information, write: Liturgy Training Publications, 1800 N. Hermitage Avenue, Chicago, IL 60622-1101.

3. Assembly

At the end of the *Design Development* phase, the architect's final version of the plans (along with a three-dimensional model if contracted for) are presented first to the planning committee and then to the larger community. This is a time for celebration as the assembly sees the fruit of the deliberations of the committee as well as their own contributions to the project. In a special and festive way the plans and model are made available to the whole assembly, along with the opportunity to hear an explanation of the designs in the light of the concepts developed by the committee and reflected upon by the assembly through the *Pre-design and Programming* phase. These plans and model, along with the concepts they express, form the basis for the fund-raising campaign for the project.

E. Construction Documents

The preparation of construction documents is the architect's responsibility. These are the "blueprints" to be used by the crafts and trades people for the actual construction of the project. Every detail of the work including the structural, mechanical, electrical, and civil engineering instructions and all materials are specified with drawings of exactly how everything fits together, down to the last screw. For a large project these instructions can easily exceed a thousand pages.

It is important to realize that it may take six weeks or more for the architect to produce the construction documents. Once they are completed with every detail checked, they are the basis for the cost estimates that will be submitted by contractors in the bidding process for the project.

Diocesan procedures govern the steps for inviting bids and awarding contracts. Contractors are usually allowed about a month to prepare a bid. Individual dioceses often have building committees that evaluate construction drawings before bids are let. The scale of the project and the architect's customary practice will govern whether a general contractor is hired to be responsible for assembling the trades people for the whole project or whether the architect oversees a series of subcontractors for specialized aspects of the work.

An alternative to submitting completed construction drawings for bid by contractors is a practice known as negotiated contracts with a contractor. In such an instance the contractor is selected prior to the preparation of the construction documents and works with the architect on materials selection and construction detailing decisions. The contractor's knowledge of materials and the newest construction techniques can be cost effective in determining the initial construction specifications. In addition, such collaboration between the architect and contractor can significantly limit the number of costly change orders which inevitably ensue. Such decisions will be worked out with the architect and diocesan officials.

F. Construction

1. Architect

When a bid has been accepted and a contract signed, the constuction begins. For a new building or a major renovation of an existing structure, it is safe to presume that it will take about a year to complete the project. During this time the architect supervises the work of the contractor, coming frequently to the site to assess the progress and to see that the construction documents are being followed. When the inevitable problems occur, it is essential that the contractor and architect quickly reach a designated representative of the planning committee in order to confer about alternative choices or to make an immediate decision. That person can then decide if an immediate meeting of the larger committee must be called or whether the decision can be made on the spot. Once construction has begun, there usually is not time to wait until the next monthly meeting of a committee!

2. Parish Planning Committee

During the *Construction* phase the planning committee has several responsibilities.

a. WORKING WITH ARTISTS

A major responsibility of the planning committee along with the liturgical consultant will be working with the artists who have been commissioned to design and make sculpture, stained glass, liturgical furniture, tabernacle, processional cross, Stations of the Cross, paschal candle stand, and other special items. The artists provide design proposals to which the committee responds. The committee then follows through as the work progresses.

b. PLANNING FOR THE RITE OF DEDICATION

The rite of dedication, presided over by the bishop, celebrates the completion of the building project and the beginning of the community's life together in the new space. The dedication of the worship space is a festive event on a major scale. The committee might begin by looking at the text of the rite (or delegating this to the liturgy committee of the parish), studying its implications, and considering how the community might best be engaged in the entire celebration. There is often a special booklet published for the dedication, which includes the liturgy, a summary of the parish's history, and recognizes the efforts made by all in the planning and building process.

G. Post-Construction Reflection on the New Worship Space

As the community begins to live in its new house and grows into spaces that are perhaps quite different from what has been familiar, both ministers and assembly will appreciate reflecting on the worship invitation afforded by the new space. This reflection might take the form of some study sessions on the rites which precede their celebration in the course of the liturgical year. Those persons responsible for seasonal environment and decoration will want to study in advance the lectionary readings and rites for the various liturgical seasons. This is done both to ensure that the seasonal decor does not overpower the ritual acts so that the ritual itself can express its power, and to enable those responsible for environment and decoration to consider how their efforts might contribute to the hospitality extended to all. The musicians will likewise want to look at the rites and lectionary readings to envision how they might lead the community's prayer in the new space.

5 Worship Places with Special Needs

There exist worship needs beyond those of the typical parochial situation, particularly in cathedrals, health care facilities, chapels for religious communities, and university chapels. Requirements particular to the assemblies which gather in these places make some demands that are out of the ordinary. Because these special requirements are easily overlooked, such worship spaces often become miniature churches which do not invite or encourage the kind of prayer most appropriate for that assembly.

A. Cathedrals

The diocesan cathedral should exemplify the best of liturgical worship spaces. All that has been said about the design of ritual spaces based on sacramental celebrations holds true for the cathedral as well. Here, above all, one should readily perceive the foundational role of baptism as the sacrament of entrance into the community of faith. The font should reflect the theological realities undergirding baptism: descent into the realms of death with Christ in order to be reborn and bathed in the blood of the Lamb unto eternal life. Likewise the table and ambo for the Eucharist should reflect the theology of a community of faith gathered at the earthly table of the Lord celebrating our foretaste of the heavenly banquet. These two primary ritual areas should reflect their relational primacy in the life of the assembly.

Liturgies in the cathedral represent the fullness of the diocese's worship, led by the bishop. It is imperative that the liturgical celebrations of the cathedral invite the participation of all the faithful. This requires that the assembly should be able to gather around the baptismal font easily at the Easter Vigil for the awesome rites of Christian initiation. Cathedral worship space also requires that the sacred oils for use at baptism, confirmation, ordination, anointing catechumens, and anointing the sick be displayed in a significant enough manner so that their importance to the diocesan community of faith is apparent. Expansive enough ritual space is also needed in the cathedral for the annual diocesan Rites of Election, Scrutinies, the Chrism Mass, ordinations, celebrations of silver and golden wedding anniversaries, etc. This ritual movement space must accommodate numbers of people and a variety of ritual movements without creating cavernous distances between the centers of ritual action and the assembly.

The placement of the bishop's chair and its proximity to the assembly, *presbyterium* (space reserved for the priests), and assisting ministers is also a significant matter in designing cathedral worship space. Historical precedents might suggest that the *cathedra* (chair) of the bishop should be located in the apse surrounded by the *presbyterium*. A Vatican II ecclesiology, however, might suggest that the *cathedra* should be distinct from, but in the midst of the assembly seating, and not in the apse or remotely located. Regardless of the *cathedra's* location, the least preferable solution places it behind any other liturgical furniture such as altar or ambo. The problem for a cathedral is that the bishop and his chair carry different symbolic value than the other presider's chair, which will be in the cathedral when liturgy is presided over by someone other than a bishop. When the bishop is not presiding, one could have the impression that two chairs are vying for prominence. When the bishop presides, the bishop's chair alone anchors the place for the convener of the worship. When a presbyter presides, the placement of his chair should always express his role as convener of the assembly for worship. This placement should never suggest competition with the bishop's *cathedra* or remoteness from the assembly.

If the cathedral is supposed to be the heart of the diocese, then it ought to reflect the values of hospitality, concern for the oppressed, and proclaim the justice of God within a diverse community without compromise. This may prove more difficult than reordering a liturgical worship space.

B. Catholic Health Care Facilities

Health care service stands among the most rapidly developing of the service industries. Many new medical and psychiatric hospitals, intermediate care facilities, nursing homes, and alcohol and substance abuse facilities are being built throughout the country, most with chapels.

A common practical need among these environments is a place that can be used ecumenically. Not only should the members of any Christian denomination find themselves comfortable and invited to worship in that space, but depending on the circumstances, members of other faith traditions, such as Jews or Moslems, should also find welcome. This means knowing the ritual needs for the kind of services that might be celebrated by various peoples in this place.

The diversity of worship needs by different denominations suggests that a totally flexible central space surrounded by a peripheral devotional zone might best serve ecumenical needs. Hospitality would dictate that a chapel used by various denominations would not be dominated by a tabernacle serving the Roman Catholic community alone. A distinctive reservation place for the tabernacle would better serve the Roman Catholic faithful while allowing the ritual space to be flexible enough to accommodate both the celebration of the Eucharist and other worship services. Ecumenical sensitivity calls for providing a cross without a corpus for the Protestant community, a prayer rug and compass for Moslems, the availability of various translations of the Scriptures and other sacred texts appropriate for the different communities. Dialogue with representatives of all the traditions involved will help accommodate the particular needs of these communities.

Chapels in health care facilities are used for services at which an assembly is ordinarily gathered, an assembly made up of both patients and staff people. But these chapels are also used for meditation and contemplation by individuals. Thus it is important to design these spaces to include the possibility of some privacy (for example, by sheltering the interior of the chapel from the immediate view of all who pass through the entrance lobby) while at the same time having hospitable and inviting entries.

Hospital chapels invite the presence of healing images. The ritual experience of healing is touch, particularly in the rite of the anointing of the sick. It is entirely appropriate to display prominently the oil for anointing, perhaps as part of the entry into the chapel, as a sign of the Christian community's readiness to embrace and anoint the sick even as the healing arts are practiced in the hospital for their recovery. A beautiful vessel filled with the holy oil lavishly proclaims the richness and generosity of God's mercy in the community's ministry to the sick.

Hospital chapels are often the greatest offenders against handicap accessibility. Heavy doors, narrow aisles, massive pews, no space or maneuverability for wheel chairs or gurneys, or for people with crutches or walkers, make the chapels inaccessible. Open, airy spaces that are inviting to all, flooring that can be negotiated by all, seating that does not exclude people, and adequate lighting are basic requirements for hospital worship spaces. Any devotional imagery should be easily seen (or approached when appropriate). Devotional imagery should be carefully chosen and designed for beauty, as well as for its capacity to engage the viewer in a way that allows for encounter with the holy.

C. Chapels for Religious Communities

Worship spaces for religious communities carry the same responsibilities of providing support for ritual actions and spiritual formation for the assembly as do parochial worship spaces. And the same guidelines apply. Although baptisms do not usually occur in community chapels, the community is still in need of a significant water image that anchors our common baptismal identity and provides a ritual place. Many ritual blessings, funeral rites, anointing rites, penitential rites, and word services for certain occasions are most powerfully celebrated at the water. Thus it is important that a space commemorating baptism with a vessel large enough and significant enough to contain life giving water be located within the assembly. Likewise, the place for the celebration of the Eucharist should be a dynamic ritual place. It is customary in many communities to celebrate the Liturgy of the Word with the assembly seated in one area, and then for the whole community to gather around the table for the Liturgy of the Eucharist. This more clearly reveals the distinction between the Liturgy of the Word and the Liturgy of the Eucharist, while at the same time emphasizing the centrality of the assembly's space during the Eucharist.

Communal celebration of the Liturgy of the Hours calls for an antiphonal seating arrangement with participants facing each other. Moveable seating allows for gathering the people for this prayer within the assembly space. These seats can then be easily arranged to be part of the seating for the Eucharist or other liturgical events.

Just as in a parochial environment, it is essential to make a distinction between corporate and private devotional prayer. Providing a distinct place for Eucharistic reservation and devotion apart from a place for Eucharistic celebration is important so that the difference between active corporate worship and contemplative private prayer can be respected. This need might best be served by a completely separate oratory for private prayer. The principles for locating statues of the saints and Stations of the Cross so that they might best express their purpose as opportunities for encounter with the holy are the same as those articulated in chapter 4.

D. University Newman Centers or Student Chapels

Worship spaces for student communities had best invite the most powerful worship possible, for the spiritual formation of students that occurs during these years will go with them into the parish communities where they later worship. The goal is to help establish a strong identity for each member as a baptized believer grounded in the assembly's discipleship of justice and compassion. To this end, just as in a parochial environment, it is important to have a significant "liturgical zone" with primacy of space for gathering and celebrating the Eucharist and for remembering and celebrating baptism. The extraordinary number of weddings celebrated in student chapels offers an excellent opportunity to reinforce the Christian belief that all must enter into the mystery of baptism for new life in Christ by locating the baptismal font in proximity to the entry and on axis with the altar. The bridal couple exemplifies the Christian journey in their entry procession as they encounter the baptismal waters on their way to the altar.

Completely movable furniture enables the kind of communal rites that are such an important part of student worship. The ability to gather the community around the table or around the font, or around a centrally located cross or ambo or candle or incense brazier, seated in chairs or on the floor, calls that community to affective worship that is transforming. Such flexibility is important for the kinds of retreat activities, guided contemplative prayer, and other events that are part of student liturgical life.

Because the number and range of activities is so extensive in a student community, it is essential that the main assembly space be reserved for communal ritual and that provision be made outside the main ritual area for private devotional prayer. The chapel for the reservation of the Eucharist might be a larger space than in some parish environments, accommodating large cushions for seating on the floor and perhaps some prayer stools or benches. Images of the saints, whether permanent or seasonal/occasional, should be carefully chosen for their ability to relate to real issues of students' lives and experiences.

Student ministries notoriously function on "shoe-string" budgets. Thus real care must be taken that "low-budget" does not mean that cheap or ugly decor and solutions are chosen. With some effort, inexpensive materials can express respect, beauty, honesty, and the authenticity that students deserve as much as any other community of believers. The environment for worship is a statement of the faith of the community that convenes there. The student worship space should both express the holiness of God's people who make up the assembly as well as invite them to the affective worship experiences that are most appropriate for them.

71